WILDFIRE

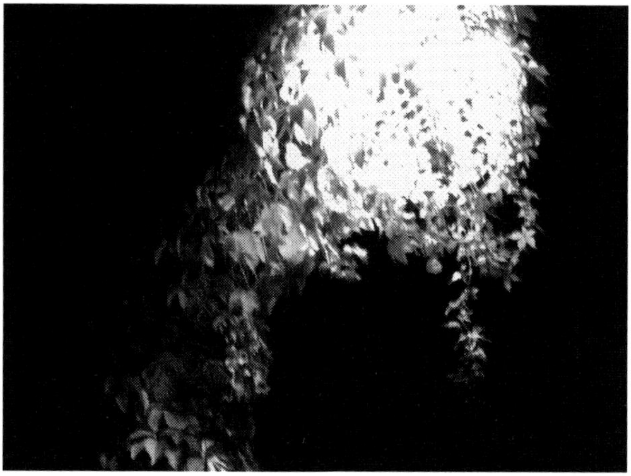

WILDFIRE

A VERSE ESSAY ON OBSCURITY AND ILLUMINATION

ANDREA BRADY

for Tom
in admiration
& solidarity
Andrea

KRUPSKAYA • 2010

ACKNOWLEDGEMENTS

An earlier version of this complete text was published on dispatx.com. Sections have also been published in the *Capilano Review* and the *New Cambridge Review*. My thanks to the editors and curators.

Cover Design: Frank Mueller
Book Design: Wayne Smith

Distibuted by Small Press Distribution, Berekley, CA
www.spdbooks.org

ISBN 978-1-928650-31-7

K R U P S K A Y A
PO Box 420249
San Francisco CA
94142-0249
www.krupskyabooks.com

Texaco motor oil, Esso, Shell, great inscriptions of human potentiality, soon we shall cross ourselves before your fountains, and the youngest among us will perish from having contemplated their nymphs in naphtha.

Louis Aragon, *Paris Peasant*

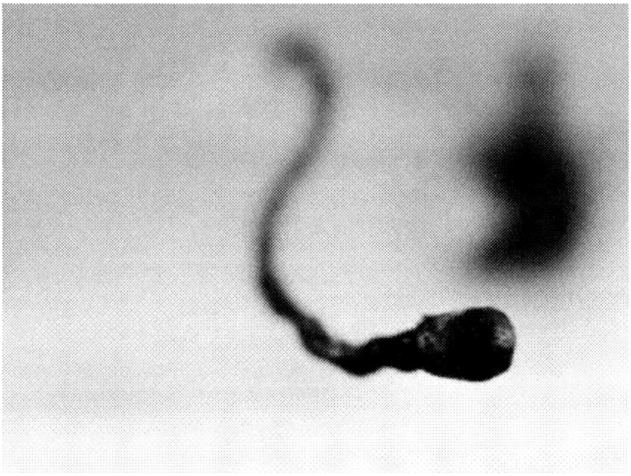

PYROTECHNE

which is to say, a cleansing

at the peat level in U Minh Thuong, man
grove and indigo, the densities
of flora which deaden radio signals
exuberant life. How can this long
advert get through

a history in which all events are the same?
By faint diffused light which remarks
steps of the travellers
through no snow on the foreground
and no crow-claw in ink; by
light filtered through a pint of blood
it links. By ire and walnut-
crusher leaning on the learner eye.

Reviewed he had to take this stand
because he was no longer covered with a skin.
Do you see what I'm saying
who is this one person the relic who wants
to know life
is getting better, depending on us
in Cau Mau, Numaniyah.
Some fanatical voices on the radio.
They don't know how right they are

to be dispersed as a mist or a foam
a text of noughts: C, P, O,
H, N, the record

conserved in the fulgent
martian head of the child of the exposed
peasant and on the helix: up five
all life climbs to air.
Thumbs the hand bearing

its light into darkest English, of history
in decay, to unlock the manufacturing
process and reveal a simple thesis
distilled for strife: that the edges
of history, past grill and lounger,
are eating inward as fire. My house
its fringe of chemical light, my child
will get sick as we all do. I am making us
a firebowl of auger of bay, to see her
is easy to see all I can I would
                                        like to call
                              your attention 'p

here's the church, here's the steeple,
open the doors and see all the people dipping
their digits into a font of automatic fire:
clothes of the damaged to be baptised in saline,
tunics of the irrecuperable can melt on them,
the congregation reads in glow of the lamb

          'if you dip a finger in it
          'it burns like a candle but produces no injury.

So open the texts, their source code a closely-guarded
state secret punishable immediate thunder.
Find what was keeping in the Bihac pocket,
the fighting compartment, abandoned

Andorinhas burned houses in the mountains
and the mountain itself. Find ourselves

in a coin war, primed to consume
the burnt, the wood, the stones, the dust,
lick up water in the trench, to pay
whatever it costs in broken vessels
drive the point away.

All things are an equal exchange
for fire and fire for all things,
as goods are for gold and gold for goods
If that is true, if money is sterile
and blood in exchange carries congenital defect,
                              all life on fire going out
                              and rekindling in a circuit:
then destruction the rule of measure in change
for moderns to circum
vent the law through a change of terms

e.g.   mark 77   mirabilis   reform
But to code in simple fricative repeat's
a copout you process the interminable present
nude with content, as if repetition were endurance.
Wildfire is tame, modified clawed
broiler and combust engine the infants of cities
though energy is natural, a fountain
arcs illumination from Texas to Medes
depending on the altruistic solar centre.
It mewls and flashes its tongue on the trays.

Fire alone can be fed, kept captive
like a vestal helpmeet, lady or return it to the wild
let fly from canisters a living payload

to prowl the brush bury in an acreage
whose future growth it claims by tender.
The Persians back their
kitchens on the large and bright, free fire,
by which clerical resistance can flow perpetually.
Rag-headed splinters drenched in the Tiber
by frenzied women. In Lebanon
they were waiting for the pitch
the tow, the puffed
Told by the CEO
to wipe the grass and young
plants in the dog days, we bury our hopes
in autumn

rain begins to fall, earth takes
its fire to all the inhabitants. As if the planet
were a woman, living, turned against us,
and the stars pin-hole cameras in a lacquer of burning
bark around a tree . . .

I have tried to make in a month what the sun
accomplishes in a year as in the brass sphere,
an excess, believing

if in fire we are in our element
then something can displace us,

that the hope is in
the recitation

I might find not fire
but thick water

bright lights
neon lights
phosphere
big city
lights
city
bright lights
neon lights
phosphere
big city

TUNIC

1.

Remember I am
on fire
cannot be trusted.

The lending librarian cut from plasticene and toffee
knows the dewey decimal place
where Greek myth can be pulled out of ravel.
This morning a reader's pass
will get you
into trouble
now the government has turned bibliographer
the living archive mutated into a bird.
It's no trouble, a caution and a few hours
answering questions about your fantasies
prove no flight risk you hop out
from stone to stone on stichomythic feet.

The ache comes back on renewal:
you cannot live here, you belong to a different crowd
you won't save unless you pay from the gut.
But the future can see underground, its eyes
make their own light flash
along tracks where everything you've done
blinks off like a solar-fired alarm.
If the living are still here
it will find and add them to the census
which you'll find filed down by the past.

Inspectors rely on repeated structures
to make sense of the chaos of competing forms
that fall on cars and coffins, no wonder
foreign dying looks so simple,
slipping skirts of flesh in antique profile
like the geometry of Muslim wallpaper.
We go together. Rectangularise the cornered.
If I tell the one about the Byzantine armies, promise
not to believe that we are all human,
that I saw them walking on newsprint in Fallujah? Then

Of the two donors, the doctor
ceded to his poisoned fetlock, forethought
donated his liver and got life—
in one kill the medicine and
the heat which might preserve us
as we wait in a nest in Tora-Bora
for the samey future on which we're trained.
'So let the curling tendril of the fire
'from the lightning bolt be sent against me,
wind in savage convulse the world
the daily grind makes history and as I
wait to be seen and warned off
by an opened magazine,
consultants blame the time
on government targets blasted
from the trees of the Hesperides.
The heroic labourer has a right
to unpaid employment benefit (laughter).
The rubber tapper meek in the trees
also waits and is not known to speak.

Don't force an axe against them:
I'll need to eat them later, for
the tree of their fields is my life,

and when I am finished burn them
in envy of my self and that ash
fertilises the earth is another irony.
If I know the tree is not for meat
cut it back in defence. The land is there
to be used, without nerve
damage there is no sound of harm. If the lake
covers a gas field I suck it,
and cover the green line with
arum seeds. There is nothing here
but transfer. They mean
to burn everything, even the lungs.

2.

The hope drunk in which we dress ourselves
for a day labour gaming
with maximum power and killer graphics
taking it hard, the must-haves this autumn
whinge at the prison of the veil.
Secularism is another orthodoxy we can't shake,
to recognise the politics in fancy dress
also buries its charge under the base
though the countdown is not due to start
for you or your oldest child
or for the slaves you inherit after that.

Dress the wound in a saline solution
as the salted water rises:
fashion turns dressing from repeat
to a 'statement' of 'interest', marking the day
mine one eternal need to keep out the cold.
Garment of fire, washed in boiling water or sandia
decon foam. Judicial molestation in orange one piece

or Walmart sweatshirt made by the guest
workers in Vietnam, 'seeds of war in the outfits
'we array by the full-length mirrors of Beximco
and Daewoosa. In the grove of war hangs
a fleece of recycled Coke bottles,
boob-tubes and desert grades making out
the farthest voyage from Sunrise Exports
of Mumbai is inevitable. We can do no more
vote with our feet dragged over the gap
to Νίκη, though in the docks
they tell of ears floating on the surface
and a chin like a monkey's in the wash.

The consumption loop *is* politics,
potential flash points all down
the supply chains the head
stepped on lights
her gown before her maid knew what was happening.
Everywhere she goes she makes
money. Can we break the news of repetition
vulture supposed of 'nowhere' the target liver
returning to the impact to look for any
growth are given the shirt off their backs
washed out by tide, released from a burden
of fertility and insecticide by a little powder
the tick-tock waves the motive, the distance

3.

By 'accident' and 'sacrifice' we have heard
how the irrational like a bunker-buster
reaches the deepest dugout.
But reason for penetration
is a substitution also countenanced by revenge:

it's ok, it's only a story and the detention
of its I they recommend indefinite.

Come closer. The doting wife
burps Tupperware, robes the patriarch
but his sacrifices overstimulate the sexual charm.
She has kept too much aside for an uncertain
future, and watches the body she meant
to cherish turn to batter in its lining.
The introversion of sacrifice that chars
other countries begins with this one,
spent after his labours to be kept close to home.
The janitorial sub-contractor rips himself to you.

Our family is also known to worship the well.
Our turn to nominate the victim is magic
as a campaign donation gives vulture funds
for reconstruction. They choose life
incense the flame, the father a pillar
or a blue tongue reaching towards heaven,
and reap the substitute teacher held
captive in a bunker of volumes.
The magician votes the word supplies
where bodies were bungled in a sundried wrap.
And though the beloved cannot be blamed,
though Medea is known as the foundress
of medicine in an oil-rich state, I am not
complete in horror if I suppose
she did feel sorry finally.

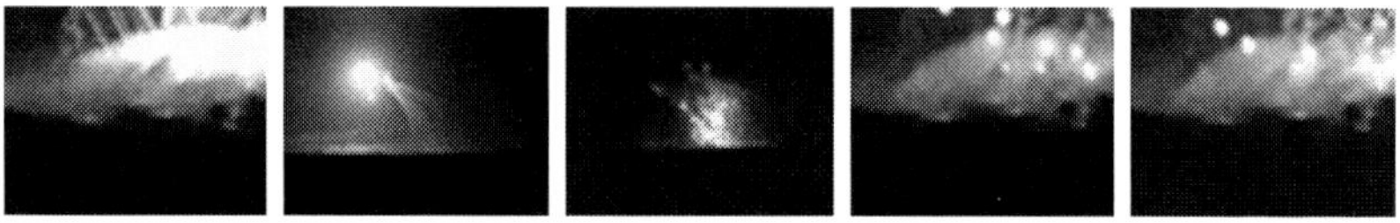

CHRONIC

. . . left flesh and bone
On many a flinty furlong of this land.
Also, the country-side is all on fire

1.

Was the god talking, or pursuing,
on a journey, or asleep?

The only way out a sea of flames

You lot: rush yourself out of here
tomorrow

2.

The earliest publications were coin. Publication
as drift: ships loaded with potential,
resinated drawn on currents
towards the tortoise towers, helepolis, piers
lapped in the dark. Propulsion
by *toxon* and bronze spout collapsed distances
formerly concrete, traducible only by wheels
or machines powered by calories, into nothing:
couplets inseparable by any moral force
more actionable than geometry. Now in syndicated repeat
the 'brutal crackdown' in Erbil exacted by its geocoordinates
(3412N/04401E), Dohuk (3625N/04301E)
these sites visible from space aflame their ground
cover: nothing lives underneath, pyrotechne

converts all that is solid into feed, and at Oak Ridge
they make the bacteria which eats even that.

Now it's easy to reach the target, unbearably
precise the nozzle turns the snout sniffing puckers:
I see you there. I consume you in a burst.

Take five and drop them . . . but who knows his mind,
The Syrian runagate I trust this to?
His service payeth me a sublimate
Blown up his nose to help the ailing eye
vases of quicklime and white lily, scented to consume the air
herald of the resurrection of the ambiguous
winner from Baalbek who cooked up the original, prop
to the dead man of Europe—guarantees defeat
of Luitprand of Cremona,
surrender of the Russian idea to another
empire with no life left in it either. Brand
heating his own modern piss, sold by Kraft
to the crowned heads for writing 'Domini'
illuminating paper. 'how beautiful
'all our centuries can be garlic bloom
integuements and pork powders and invisible ink:

A good time for the industrious, until a shortage
of beer and milk bottles hit the happy, the baby.
After the retreat of the shamed Diodachi the weapons
scattered on the highway of death were sold
to finance the building of the Colossus, pillars of Hercules,
double bars struck through a glowing S:
twins remembered by scorchlight on anniversary.
The peripherique manacles these victories,
monuments the spoils of survival too bitter
to be named for itself caress the air at the centre,
whose bricks also listen to the dead. Baghdad destroyed

by the naffatoun in their asbestos shirts,
learning from the 30,000 lost to a sickened Byzantine parade
the irrelevance of numbers. In 683
lighting the kiswah, splitting the black stone in three pieces
a triad of opposition solidifies over its middle,
an axis through which enmity radiates,
terms of concession, obliteration and raw nerve.
Sizzling through fat and liquid, pausing finally on the bone
                                        shake-n-bake guy
                                        puts me off
                                        my pork crackling
The more life a thing has, the less it can defend itself
thickened with soap trying to be clean of
my hair began to singe in the public lavatory

3.

While researching 'weapons for the burning of armies'
by report: 30,000 men of the Muslim navy, Kyzikos 680.
35,000 houses in Fallujah but not a one among them.
From '54 in Algeria, through Attrition in the Delta.
The Jordan. Durazzo. 'Rome on her march
'to stamp out like a little spark thy town Grozny
the Seventh Crusade at Syllaeum or against the Vikings in 941
and in translation: occasions the first Arabic medical textbook in Basra
the album of the poisoner above.
Even the stone tomb of Moses releases what distilled
like rose water in the alembic burns
hotter than wood. Bombarded
by naphtha arrows, mangonels and flake
'so entertaining I have to smile ablaze white-turbaned
'the falling trunk and limbs, the crash, the muffled shriek, the groan
suicide squads pumping the dead smoke and trench full of horses
in Acre 1291, templars best known for defeating

church policy on usury and for services to capitalism
'They can indeed be soldiers of Christ blood for bitter wine
rubbled under burning, sublimate
to the medieval air. Pledge
look up to Beau Seant, financiers
locked in fealty to the company
to their desks in floors above the impact.

Gawain locked in single combat for Jerusalem.
He who conquered the technology of fear ended
the age of heroism leaving an instinct unemployed.
Battling degraded the city resembles Chicago,
its walls wailing, its night of the mount continuous
limit of our decay for strauss and rose,
unspeakable cures by the smokes
of sacrifice and longing that light
the napalm that pulverises leaves. On the home
front strongholds of clay and waddle and steers'
skins draped over the city walls to forestall fire:
and undoubtedly the mechanization of laughter
hanging upside-down from a line
that circles from hell back into morning glare.
In stockyard light to see
as if by day the camp, our own people

4.

Fragmentation set off among the fire-fighters,
each piece has designs on an individual
but the movement of the avant-garde
plans to enrapture whole cities
lends to the shade the appearance of shining.

Embed Darrin Mortenson reports 'the boom
'kicked the dust around
'the pit as they ran through the drill stern efforts
to avoid cracking, came on to them
like a vinegar-cask the noise the sexual

like thunder spearing fire from perronels
fully orchestrated to cause notional breakdown.
Beards singed but not much
injured for sake of being
on their knees in prayer at the time sold
to Louis XV in 1756, saltpetre, turpentine,
tallow that carcass composition rosin, crude
which may be deemed excessively indiscriminate
like history into which it all disintegrates
the Congreve rockets glaring down on McHenry
make the top-ten forever

Discourse to him of prodigious armaments
Assembled to besiege his city now,
And of the passing of a mule with gourds—
antimony nights of wrath and ashes, the Greek Fire
of another translation of faith 'burnt to dust and ashes
'the centuries of the middle ages, . . . with their poetry
'and lack of thought, birthing the time of the public,
Napoleon, and *la puissance du journalisme.*

I see the genius of the modern, child of the real and ideal,
Clearing the ground for broad humanity, the true America, heir of the past so grand,
To build a grander future
also in soft drinks, and toothpaste.

5.

Anything organic can be drawn, calcined
for days on the stove, from this need for gold.
Hot bones. Slick from the periodical table,
degreased by the Danube.
A history of deception and trade
secrets, spirit of fireflies trapped in pine
or growing with age and envy to a hoop,
the nature sits there waiting to be discovered.

Then patents apply: Sweden
forested with matchsticks, lights to secure the hold
of ships from burning
sandwiched in the enmity of elements, sealed in glass
bulbs to attract fish, to illuminate the hands
of clocks and sweated workers, to guide mowers
by living lamps and courtesy, to represent
friendship with the dark

classes. Next in Denmark a fiction dies
hallucinating turkey,
plum puddings, and shooting stars.

                    Marie Jankovitz, her power to eat and speak
'faded away as they had been petals of a fading flower,
labour,
tarnished and pointless, repeating
by the dip-tanks, venerate the compo,
infused in illumination under the low ceiling.
Is this labour, pinks
unfading perennials, tarnish its aim:
by return to uncover what in the composition—
that nothing turns on illumination
the Delphi women were just high on ether
and Princess Ida's college full of wet matches
singed their fine Linnen with the bedtime exercises,
that the process, though plain, cannot say so . . . ?

Cyril. Fancy, a hundred matches—all alight!—
That's if I strike them as I hope to do!
Gama . . . . strike their teeming brains,
And not their hearts. They're safety matches, sir,
And they light only on the knowledge box—

Quakers in Oldbury, free of the Test,
learning by experience to legislate and use
the coal, the alkali to break faith
with absolute conviction. Or model
Gothic on Fairfield Row, arched and turreted
so completed the blight. Their emblem the ark,
secure profit even by light,

‘a natural and beautiful image even
‘in these days of neon and the hologram.
George Fox dreamed of infinite ocean, ‘of light
‘and love, which flowed over the ocean of darkness,
the light which ‘shines on in the dark, and the darkness
‘has never mastered it. The stacks
changed the night to concert, the birds
driven by industrial choirmasters to up their piece-rate . . .

The chocolate-maker, Darby the smelter found profit
in red glare. John Woolman declared
against wars walking in light: ‘may we look upon our treasures
‘and the furniture of our houses, and the garments
‘in which we array ourselves, and try whether the seeds
‘of war have any nourishment in these, our possessions.
The Children of Light developed reputations for honouring
contracts and selling quality goods, for industrial experiment,
factories like minor cities full of the remediated.
Added phosgene to their job list. A kind of inner light
they took to the people at Cherbourg, Hamburg, Sachon.

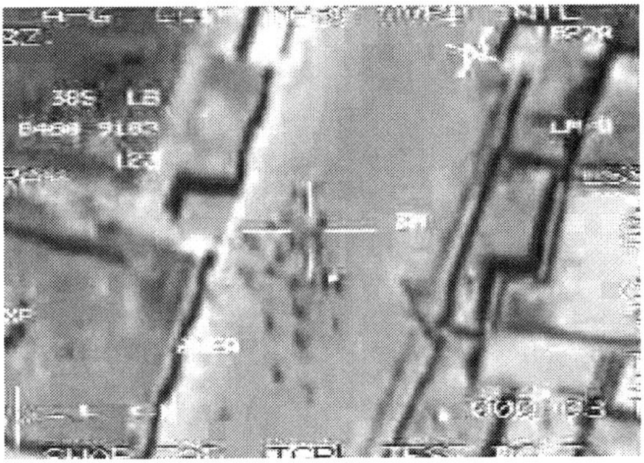

6.

In other words, we may need to
flatten Fallujah.
to destroy it.
to grind it,
pulverize it
and salt the soil, as the Romans did
to make an example (Joseph Farah)

'Viscous, not unlike the Gum of Cherries,
'and some others newly taken from the Tree:
the contractors "debased" on a bridge in March
are rich fruit gone off and strange turn
cherry-bombs stink out Pallugtha.

32 seconds to contact; the audio tell aw dude.
Hit him; hit the truck and him; the truck
in the subject is part of him, violate mechanisms.
You who we see who is spoken to
a vapour, a phantom fury
writes with 'a more blazing
'and pleasant flame shooting
downwards through the Jolan precipitate,
brings light along the trench line
(if lyrics could be sewn with razors),
and bites all the legs in the spider-holes,
and bites the long tucked tail of smoke.

   Keeping the 'house of Satan'
   cruciform in chaos, tipped MDF panel
   on lineoleum, or floral ticking, an arm lock
   as if it could be wind
   a watch or stick up a dozing head
We recharge our batteries in Dreamland,
get the hygiene stuff at the PX, watch
boat races of stiff young coxes with their whole lives
Egyptian cotton from the university. Stone bridge
with white lamp-posts on the island tends
the *lumen naturalis* through the sanded night.
Look at the race. Now can we look

at the dead postures of accident,
their homes, their stuff
looked at them also. A rubber sandal. Plates.
A white surrender. The ulcerous Aleppo button.
The leather casing of a face, dented
like a football. Invert skin continues
the body beyond the fingertips, *collapsed*
concrete distances into nothing, now distance
is nothing, the alternatives spin web-

reports of illegal weapons you can almost touch them
into nothing but sloppy joes. This dead girl
is trying to hold your hhhhhh her palm
a pilgrim into air, a vapour, a breath away.
The niggers of the dunes. Salted
ash from the braai does the job on the earth
oh my Romans, to sell
at Sanctuary in Covent Garden.

Eaten by dogs. viewed: 36,560 times.
Eaten by dogs. viewed: 17,809 times.
Person with disability: prosthetics above body.
Partially eaten by dogs. viewed: 32,144 times.
Old man killed with daughters; family recognised. viewed 30,411 times.
Man making "Shuhada" sign: there is
one God, because he knew he was
about to be shot. viewed 18,135 times.
No comment. viewed: 23,455 times.
Man killed at home, identified. viewed 13,759 times.
The spirit of violets cannot wash the floor in green
or relieve blood jammed up in an eyeball: it complains,
every time you piss you are pissing in its socket
it is a drunkard whose thousand orifices new-modelled
are the American drains.

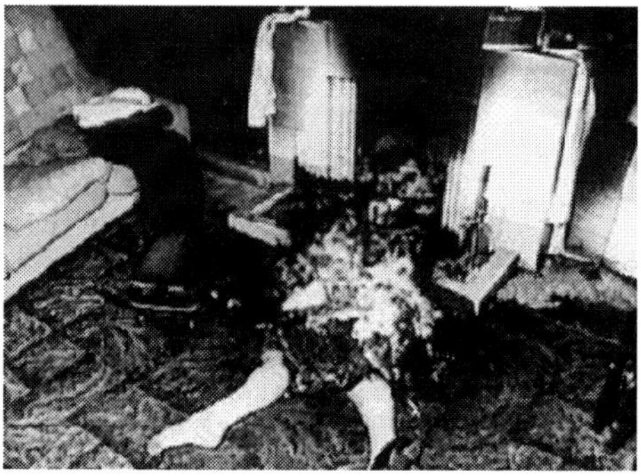

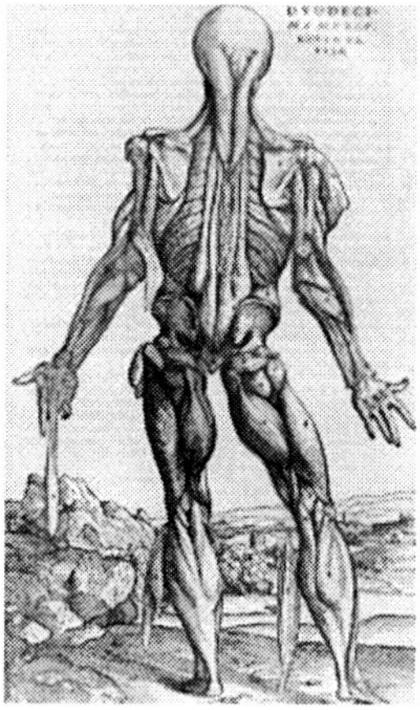

MEAT

"Although mathematically it can be shown that the human body contains enough energy stored in the form of fat and other tissues to consume it completely, in normal circumstances bodies will not sustain a flame on their own."

1.

So much fat for soap in seven cakes on a spatula,
with burnt lipids or boneash making a fine organic spectacle,
the composition flourishes in a sheltered spot.
It is just mass. A number. Nothing special.
'If we admit, with many Learned Moderns,
'a flamma vitalis in the heart . . .

Again again foaming in the washhouse, the bedroom
where all obscurity ceases under cover
ecstatic fumbling with masks . . . have a letter-press
invitation to witness

the girls strip off and curse their indulgences
          (the handlers are prone
          to venereal excitation)
as fat is especially likeable to the custom

                    eats itself into the life of life,
          As saffron tingeth flesh, blood, bones and all!
          For see, how he takes up the after-life
          dressed in salt to prevent his skin reigniting

little marks he brought back, the pins, shark tooth
keloids form a collar are ethnically selective
                                        Meaning the wound coils
black nut purged from its catkin a lacquer

shell the head is fathomless
look down the bridge of your nose at your brain
quietening its steady chatter. Ride out
the monkey mind. The fullness of time
is deceptive, the ignition skin a bit more grey than usual.

Restlessness, hallucinated
contacts between meanings
I can feel the structure giving way
needing treatment, a liquid
to massify the gaps
become giddy, anxious, you get
confused, convulsing, hard
breathing
sweat
thirsty

cramp and piss: the iris of your eye closing
losing reception,
body without outlet,
closed, afraid of a photo, lacrimating.
Bereft of greens, nothing but pain is left what
can you see out there
in everything? No stupid.
Richness, blazing even under water.
Clouds of ash on the perimeter. A biosphere.

2.

All of which will be forgotten, she
said, sweeping her arm across the city.
All that human diversity a plate of embers, 'with a likeness
'burst in memory preserved in by-products of insect death.

The ability to harm is limited by stupidity.
From Lincke at the Golden Lion you could have caught
your death in gold or silver capsules.
But death slips gilded through the colon
without ever sipping air. 2,200 matches

cursing a live feed, tripwire around
entry points for basic information on the body,
the literal point of entry
is small and precise in the neck for these enfolds
compare skin where chicken nuggets bark and fry.
In a precise manner what man is made.

A wick effect leaves the foot
of Mary Reeser
untucked, the sequence so mysterious
it makes death more curious than generic.

And for daily workers an assault on the jaw,
days follow the bitter taste of sequestra
eating, talking, consolation dissolve
before anything nudges the radiogram. The myth
of one a highlight for the big dipper

drinks his way out of melancholy and stink
Santogen tonic wine and white lightning,
delayed healing troubles the practice

nurse on her home visits reads a bottle of urine,
or at least domestic effects
should pay for our emissions. Days after the encounter

skin still flashes like a refinery seen from the express,
like bargain xmas lights loose on stolon.
A firm eschar surrounded by vesiculation is the key
hole in a canvas whose surface is made artistic by its destruction,
wet and sticky explorations of the inner body

with knife back, finding I had lost the capacity to feel
                                        his body is his answer
much more than relief as I turned on my life
rough dunked in the tunic salt-water. The hands meant
to help me bursting also into flame
who might leave nothing but a foot in a slipper.

ALCHEMISTRY

1.

          and after the recitation found
that in coffee sweet with splenda
I have been displaced

I am a kind of sucrose, a walking
salt-cellar, unexpired match
bodies assembled properties
with industrial uses, so we can belong
to the logic of mechanized labour even
as deep into this study as
I am from a mass movement.

All solids melt to air, dust
resettles as dust, we can still be useful
like the cremaines in the egg timer,
or Anne King yielding by weight, the text charged
to audit each Grane and Atome of relief.
In time. Pissing to the wind

we miss a target cycle: the leaves, the marrow
pass through the human tube with some
of their manichean light still shining,
an armoury / an entrepreneur are waiting
to collect our excess and feed the fire.

Consumption frees energy and vapour
bound with steel wool, or gas released
by instant charges appropriate

wherever there is water, there is life,
foaming with light, the eddy is vital
clue to the confusion of an animal world.
Space is its limit, contains its impossibility.

The greens who say the future's humanure
make waste a historical tie-in,
but the dream of total expenditure without redemption
is an open market where we can detonate:
over fields of blé, militant clouds
pose another challenge for the cyanometer,
the search for all possible initials
driven to extinction, and thus discovers californium.

With the powder dry references scatter,
but we began with somewhat that belonged
to the body of man…

2.

For the aetiology of phosphorescence
substitute bone. For lightness substitute ash.
Bone, or human water, or all organic matter
lain in a great heat can shine on in the dark
or bring tactical darkness to conflict.
At the bottom of a glazed earthenware jar
closed carefully with philosophical lute
there is bone, and bone belongs to ash.
Bone softened in acid,
its liquour treated with milk
of lime, washed and dried; bone
closed in a body of philosophical lute
gives itself up to an instrumental ministry.

If the timing is right, the know-how
it can be sublimed

and to encourage amplitude and reflection,
thermal penetration, the advice is use

                    more if he is distant.

'The mass must be stirred
'at mid-day, with care, the body protected
'kept from the sun until it is wanted.
'Engines smeared in the evening,
'at sunrise all will be burnt:
such recipes are magical, really pretty evocative,
but primitive and the effect is wanting.

Rock forms cast into wedges with the extra
gypsum sold to strengthen the fields, acid
dried in iron pots and flung on faces.
Albright at the slaughter-houses of Galați
the bones too noisome to ship, or the crews
did not survive   a furnace
to feed the British scene, banked in Russia, Morocco,
Florida, Tennessee apatite,
Caribbean Sombrero, West Indian
Redonda, or Charleston; white
or yellow, red, black or violet, as it darkens
it becomes less dangerous to its handlers.
But must still be wrapped and tanked under water,
water-boarded but treated with dignity.

                    more if he is distant.

As it dissolves in the same water it absorbs
it is a model of antiperistasis, a pump-primed cycle
bulks its efficiency, pound for pound.
In principle opposites
replace each other until both are spent,
less dialectic than mutually-assured gavotte,
leaving casualties with a bad throat: all that's left
of politics is an evacuation,
and all that's redeemed is pulp
at the end of the tumble
that schoolkids can use to make paper.

3.

Accepting loss turns to giving. What's
the matter is hygroscopic, like honey,
ethanol or glycerine, gifts of the three sovereigns
for marriage, blindness and bakery.
The early chemists bashed it out essentially,
their brute solutions displaced
for a double order on the fireworks
of nostalgia and Scott Key. Their lists
magical, poetical, dependent
on linseed or laurel oil.
The power of obscurity to bring it all
to life. Who

said powder
said fire

The search for a purer fire recedes
deep in the angles of history: wildfire,
a boy's own myth, its obscurity fastidious
as its composition unknown:
        concocted oil, sulphur, resin, willow
        charcoal, sale nitro, aqua vitae, and camphor
the hectic business of the living day
        bitumen, slaked lime,
collect the death certificate from the
        bones, charcoal, lithium,
and wrap and pacify the spirit in Ethiopian wool
        sodium, incense, tow,
        paste of talc, eggwhites, gum, and salamander
whose skin is our asbestos and her disease
        powdered aconite root, monkshood, magic
        beans, arsenic, hemp for hallucination,
receipts for the secret of angels
        blister beetles, rock salt, incense, thunderbolt stone,
        ground in a black mortar in the mid-day sun,
the elemental found in combination
        mixed with resin of the black sycamore
        and liquid asphalt of Zakynthos to a paste
indentures industrial workers and other janissaries
        a talcum of phosphorous pentoxide: whiskey pete
bunching overhead like men o' war, luminous, ballooned
bellies 'not wan from Asia's fetiches
        with quicklime, syrupy liquid removed calcium
        by nitric or sulphuric acid
        reduced by ignition with carbon
all variation is a mark on a paper, by a worker
hoping for even numinous reward.

// said powder
// said fire

And what is left to say. Those wars are over.
This war a target cycle, feeds itself
on water and air, and will outlast us all:
for science an arrow burns perpetually
in all bright rhetoric and in clouds
a treachery of movers looks just elemental,
dust returning through fire to its resting.
In its pure state a body is clear as optical glass,
refractive index like a diamond
hard, beautiful and almost incapable
of succumbing to mechanical pressure.
But it is only ever found in combination.

4.

So we await patiently the results of the inquiry,
and stand far behind Kyoto, in shadow.

Fierce Feavers must calcine The Body of this World:

and there will be a reward at the end
for those who can continue

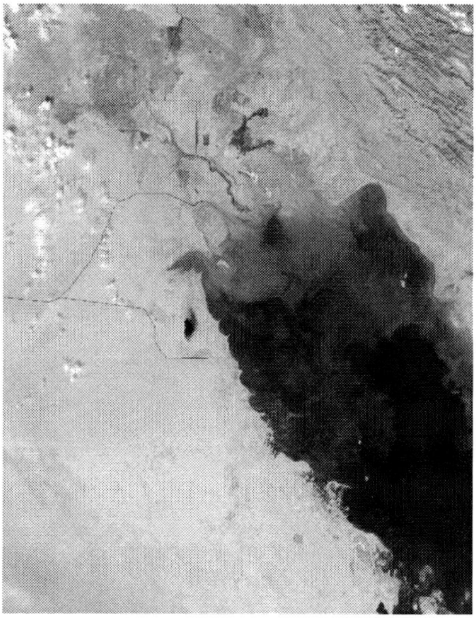

CRUDE

This is automatic fire.
This is automatic fire, a token ring

each extruder talking English to themselves.
The technology driven since 4 BCE
by carpooled naptha 'you know
'their backs which are dark   and evil-smelling
the dark night of the well anyway
we have always been like that
milking the fabled white worm of Punjab
stuffing the carburettor with chip fat
heavy and burning for it, the marshals
bowing deeply at the wells of Baku to the energy
and ideals upon which the Nation was founded.

Counterfeited gluttony as medical fire, oil of Persia
its lifeblood rid of hope and freedom
when explosions flash along the street like bunting.
Used as patching, to blacken insipid inks. From it
we take our English word that overspill
coats the wings of seabirds and coughs
their little throats down, all the shores
make a circle for the broadcast. Trade goods distilled
as liquid fire that runs into the thousands
of syllables of a world order duped by RepRap,

and runs the little heaters in poor homes.
I dried my curls before the soph hop,
came aspiring into the night perfumed like a pick-up;
and often woke to see it creeping under the door
as we lay dying, the wick gasping
for its dangerous life, my rayon pyjamas

flashing with static charges that blued
the petrochemical pale. For which reason
avoid Vaseline, which is obscene, especially for lips,
and keep the window open all through winter.

In oils danger-close relate to fire,
which leaps upon it from anywhere as soon as it beholds it
and stuns the leg, and stuns
a girl in her nightgown in Haditha.
Gas flown overhead into safety as the wind
blows the drone away. A lob would suffice
to bring the nature of this appetite in close,
what fine traces it ribbons
through the mezzanine, that dark wish
between two fronts. On the home
front a pen of sparklers writes apocrypha
and recipes on the body of the state-
sponsored torture artist. Fame
hides her in the fragrant rich
bosom of the Arabian mountains, but she
flies haughty through our own skies, untaxed
for the vapour which zips our joint intemperance
the ariel bombers, the cargo flights that cross
above the cradle of history become a sink.

I love what I hate
and can't stop drinking,
shooing out the windows, pumping it
into my lap. It fills life automatically
and makes that life an odometer.
You know that, it's your mango, radio,
factoid in the siphon, but we are automatic
fire our reps with Nectar, and landscapes.

THROWN FIRE

You are now entering the marshes:
no kite-flying beyond this point.

Smeared with crows flown against the tents
flies away suddenly to whatever place you wish
burns up everything. Vectors born
in nectar by the Nile piggyback birds
make way to New York, swimming in encephalitis.

How can a wish,
wishing even to destroy, transport itself.
By falarica, and fire-flutes played slowly
towards the target so that the bitumen melody
can flicker along the fortified register.
By Howitzer, in a 155 mm shell, and hand
grenades, built to appeal to the hand
like an American football, degenerate
son of *mikroi siphones*. Or hurling jars.
The story of ballistics is convection
of spite. When nothing else will traverse
the dangerous gap between owned and aspired,
and evacuation still seems necessary, fire.
The origin of human flight is not birds.

To avoid the pent-house the Saracens
shot straight up into the clouds,
their darts fall back on top of them,
their bodies, houses that move
now only language. Kept off by tourniquet
and perronel, hailed by angelic technique
rocks and timber baulks, a hundred stealth

taxes under labour. The caliph
of Damascus with his blatant equipment,
the refining explosion pulled back
on credit by international inspectors
is redeployed by rational actors on the north stage.

Clearance of one organisation to its opposite
is known as no man's
land is all the difference
between loyalty and hate. The whites
of their eyes—pseudo-intimacies of the machines,
the pocket-mark on a body infused
with the differential breath of aerosols.
Opposites critiqued, alarming
Ktebisios' double-acting piston, replaced
horses plunging desperately into water
but the logic of elemental opposition has finally reached its end.
Though the danger of the instability of our weapons
sometimes results in friendly fire consumption
of the whole deck, we stick by our strategies,
or stick like melted candles to the table.

Fused like the forked legs of the animal,
a structure designed chronometer
recharged by shaking. Or a fuze
barrette that knows the rider
is in the air, or got sufficiently older,
helps us to see how time's the interval
to the airburst: and we might go
in yellow. Our little pointless arrow
brightens as it goes over. While it shines
we remain harmless.

Then sinks the object in darkness.
Phosphor a beacon to the resurrection men

agenting the trenches, to the infantry
on a slippery bank following their
strafing—into bush, rock ornamental
motion and heat the human signs—
like the would-be Romans spying on Carthage
from inside a smoke of Venus. And the queen,
what she could see through the smoke
she clears herself, hiding her gaping
expectation behind the privacy glass of heroic death
which neither blocks the image nor reveals it.

Screened, blocked, scared, on the move
at a crawl within the smoke an armoured city.
Used to limit his vision, his access to his ammunition.
And if I were to use that language—a mode
that absorbs its screening mass from the atmosphere
of commerce, politics and waste, from the family
and the strangers in no one man's land
to work or friendship, thinking only of themselves,
that takes up its position in bright balloons
could grow infinitely given a will and a hand,
an output hot, white and dense—
have I scored a blinder, or run blind
myself in all this vapour quickly spending
its burn I think I'm seeing the future?

Mass extinction of smokes, relative tenacity
depends on the ambient moisture, the life
that can be lived even in banks of sand.
Fight to hold a gap that might not even be contested.
Kissing E. B. Hershberg's plunging rod
surrounded by phosphor, and by napalm
like an ice-cream sandwich or an experimental
poem dashed onto political density:
the insert from Save the Children fragments

the cloudy raiment of late-industrial processing,
the gas scatters, inflamed, but as there is nothing
here worth burning we are off the hook again.
And left in the artist colony, attached to a hose
of advantageous melancholy be sure
your mouth is clear before the stolen gas rises
in the siphon. So to continue.

For what it's worth fighting for brass
with a legendary mischief, right
as rain might get beaten
back or just dissolve our hopes like sugar.
15% in the charred wedge lives to fight again,
the rebel army pins its hopes
on the nugget of information secreted
under the emperor's skin. He is a blue torch
in the last scene, when all our colonies are destroyed,
and we a band of villains with some ancient fliers.
I aggrandise myself among them. Belonging to me
as good belongs to you in theory, blown
by violent and continuous breath
  shadowed by the obscure precision
of the typewriter, rigidly translating the spaces
left open in the *liber ignium* of Marcus Graecus.

SECURITY

IN LAW

1.

The case for flying fire
The case for making thunder

                unrestrained, it drops
as a gentle rain from heaven upon the place beneath,
Safwan Hill, swabs the river and canal there.
A new name covers it: mark there,
oil displaced by kerosene is 'no great way to die
'but the generals love it. It has a big psychological effect
a history of pity and the smell of victory
flashes burning the breathed into the breather,
a child at cross-purposes heading the other way
in shredded lettuce, dressed sort of uh aioli.

Fire plays on the mind, as if its form depends
on imagining the toxic effects that breach nature's
Genevan protocols, to depend on its toxicity, to cause
                through chemical action
            temporary or permanent harm
    humans or animals
the wrong hands ablaze the humans come
to an animal end in snuff shots too tough
for prime time if not walking on
real estate. But the stocks had already fallen

anyway, from the eyes, in the extraordinary
enclaves of Cuba, cremated
at Rocketdyne, or donated

to the kilns by Fallbrook.
The potential for recombination is sublime,
too hard to legislate the patent
resourcefulness of medical doctors:
we can always remediate their sticky ends,
work through the scars in the parchment
with its Leagueish will to contain fire and harm . . .
        'designing to attack persons with fire,
        'not to give light or to be luminous
        'or to lighteth every man that cometh into the world,
        'or to walk as children of light, to profit by that

Light is everything, is the opposite of fat, is relish
without coping

Law promethean, expectation
bound not binding.

2.

Are law's best or worst meanings concealed
in wood, barbed, poisoned, the points blazing with fire?
My paper is bogus—no pre-nup is airtight,
and its mark holds you in confusion as its proof-weight
of harmlessness. The wicked speak clearly,
broad-faced as the court of appeals, so is obscurity
a moral option now? Danger
burns up the outside, and in no wind
fire sucks in upwards from tenements like a stove-pipe
build to the power of a hurricane to pluck
pedestrians from their circuits redecorating
the communal stairwells in double grey.
From the echelon it is hard to see a raged city plan.

So what is 'too murderous' to the lateral council
anyway to use incendiary agents
against targets *requiring* their use,
you asked for it, I am not violative
of law, the law of land
warfare, we are just delegates to a different conference
tongue slower than bullets.

The coward strikes a bald head,
and a tyrant ages flying hair with charcoal;
the ambassador without portfolio sits down, says "I am thine",
links his fortunes by watered recrimination to the attaché
opening up new causeways through the interior.
Danger gets the crystal mark for official clarity,
the truth a category of prisoners asleep, naked,
spectating, broken, afflicted and grievous, in fear or flight . . .

But for the apocalypse they give us the freedom
of information act, and for 2d five sparrows: that nothing
concealed will not be revealed, filmy nothings
said in the darkness heard in the light,
whispers in doorways proclaimed on the ridgepole.
As Liam Fox's explanation is a brutal weapon,
                    but we need to remember
                 that we were talking
                    about some pretty brutal insurgents.
A sheen of bolt truth lies boldly over the details,
two categories of happening, both of which make me afraid.
These are the gradations of obscurity in public discourse,
our work the endometrium that binds the naked surface
to a dark displaced richness of fact
which may or may not sustain the future.

3.

Believing persecution is greater than slaughter,
that it builds the organisation in the long run
you'll never make in that slip and trainers:
these are people, hoping they might evolve to be more
than numbers. Inmates. Waging asymmetrical war
in their jumpsuits   might dream of the fire
they're in as an airfield
in Bagram, we just can't know for certain
what intentions in their rat hearts
their sports drinks.

Like they told us the rules of our engagement with the dunes:
i. feed the people poisoned rice and water for the gods;
ii. lie concealed in a hole bored into the body of an idol
after eating sacramental food and setting up an altar;
iii. lie in a secret hole in a wall;
iv. lie in a hole made in the body of an idol in an underground chamber;
v. hide fiery spies in a tunnel, or inside a secret wall;
vi. confront them at night and run down the side;
vii. loosen the fastening of a machine to fall on them;
viii. set fire to their rooms smeared with poisons and explosives,
or made of lac;
ix. slay them in pleasure parks and places of recreation;
x. get out disguised as a heretic with his retinue;
xi. get out disguised as a woman following a corpse;
xii. get carried off by spies as a corpse. Women
xiii. may throw a snake, or poison, or fire or poisonous smoke
over his sleeping person. Women
xiv. having access to the enemy's harem, may, when opportunities occur,
do to the enemy whatever is found possible on the occasion,
and then get out unknown.

4.

The secrets of lightning are angels',
force and friction, so struck its shareholders
anyone leaking into the marketplace
a weapon is naturally private, reticence
'a tradition of the chemical industry the compound
is not an open field for those it changes.
Constantine Porphyrogenitus reserves his rights 'nor red
'from Europe's old dynastic slaughter-house
is the stinking log-cabin of proprietary curiosity:
phantasm of ritual illuminates mouths of cows and sheep,
a new order of knowledge is here in democratic
like an ethnographer violated in a Parisian abattoir.
The structures of purity for meat replicate themselves
even at the terminal canteen, you, there, and on the cheap
flight you take to get there.

5.

We consist in a fantasy of proportionality.
So our architecture narrows to a single point.
He may do nothing but by love's leave.

LOVE'S FIRE

1.

Smothered in bitter wine or mud, heart's fire
your moist air *immo fomento alitur uberrimo*
an altogether different poison revised with kerosene
that enlightens the closed garden where she sits.
Nodding her head to the burnt heart. The lone star

states air conditioned, their walled gardens irrigated with glacial ice
while everyone burns our heads
with the desire to need—that stinkinde flesches luve
where we put the mince and the moving.

This subtle liquid fire that turns Jack
to meltwater, gathers in lipids, boils over
tongues too obligated to speak to it.
From donkey-jawed workers and plump
lipped law swillers, swaying in the doorframe
of history the holes in their bodies make against Angel,

a fountain of spontaneous relay lights:
glowing in the belly, swelling organs
making visible their breakdown in the dark
private places where they do embrace
without consequence. I want to ask my question, or break
felt into scraps the envelope in which this complex
and deepening past touches its pieces,
like the index corners of photoshopped families
all jumbled in the bladder sack together.

'But' the language slides through, dental tape
caloric fire and phosphorescence, a paper wick
dunked in subtle liquid looking like gum.
And houses turning their faces
		Make a mirrored wardrobe.
		Make this mirrored wardrobe for the

silvering. These are the halos of magic dressing, under
which my body can become a torch. It's been known
to happen. Breath extends towards man,
meets the fire on the tip and catches light and falls.
And when held inadvisably in the trouser pocket
the trousers catch on fire, scalding the walker
as he crosses towards the Chandos,
leaving a crease across his thigh.

2.

In heavy fire some saw a living element
generated in destruction, fed on carbon and fresh air,
and so a character which could breach the places
in which women sat separate, washing their clothes.
On it, life. And life buckled within it.

Distance is a communication system. Generations
of advances in artillery demolish that orange and white
intimacy, league and beleaguered, script technician
and pasteurized re-enactors from Perth,
highly energetic types that explode over water. None of which

'worldliche tribulatiuns, nane temptatiuns,
'nowther inre ne utter can sound down to a stable compound
when down is cinders. Another kind
of relation spurts through siphons
hurled over mudflat walls, P4O10,

now distance is nothing. The alternatives spin
like the iPod wheel under chapped thumbs
as the milk-blistered lips synch silently.

To desire. To appear from nowhere, always expected.
In this week's heat slummy mummies kindle it under
tank-tops, immolated virgins whip it out
in cargo and traffic, stringing pills on natural
diadems that light the air they spin like floss in.
Judge her yourself—isn't she insane?
Fame puts her away nowhere, in Arab mountains
she loads a rifle or weeps her eyes out or writes
to the directorate of football, and it is waiting
for death to explode from her zipper as she walks
downstairs from a cookery class or watches Pop Idol
pumping the crossword for a lucent meaning.
Her petrarchan look downturns the bow-shaped mouth
from which these so-called flaming arrows
gave intoxication its prettier name.
Eyes like burning casks, the only relief to smother
in vinegar, piss, or damp sand, in idleness,
in mourning for a past which was reprehensible.

But one medium-sized nail drives out another, one desire
displaced by junk food, soft hair, skin and iron.

Feeding him you heap burning coals over his head.

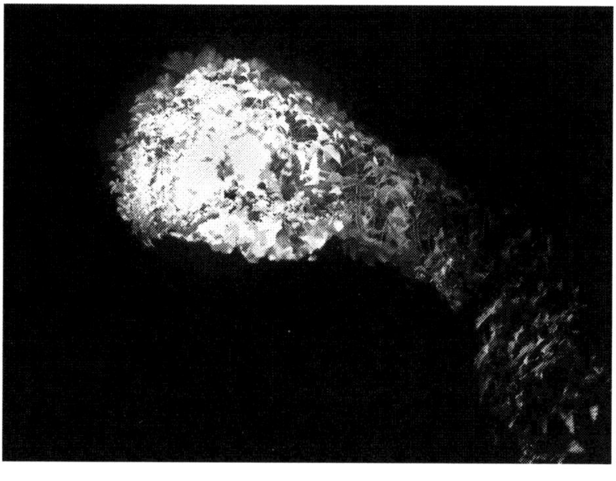

ILLUMINATED

The difficulty is not organic, meaning
you will eat through the flesh eventually and tamp down
your singularity verdict in a lucky dip. Smoke facts
obscurity a weapon snatched from insurgents
who know where it winters,
among rocks by the sunset theirs is general,
not launched into a field where his presence is made
known by the hidden particularity.

Doddery and schematic how we decline
the empire rusting, the AChE in the control
centre and finally expire paranoia in a billion particles
a curse makes the territorial managers legendary
and no-one with any wisdom will dig there,
corrugate the ceramic tooth. These are images
in a poem: tooth, rust, paranoia you may
insert your translation here, if the acquittals service
is still taking applications, and we insure they
are and know how, they have
the most recent binomial manual says
'nonidentity' when you get to the front.

That is, pound + shop, articles
for everyday life whose light
where am I myself,
where do I originate, where I die, or most transparent
in the middle, where pure, unmixed
in relief I make no show but carrying.
You carry on. You give me the shivers.

"The pure work disappears into words,
text mobilized by the shock of differences;

you light up in their reciprocal reflection
like a virtual
stream of fireworks over jewels,
restoring breath to the impulse,
the sentence." As canisters surface
from the north sea bed unchanged,
neither salted nor strange, and nostalgia
glows meekly over the Fourth. Your sentence
is new and runs consecutively,
you weigh it, minding the wishes
for a pearl, a win, restored breath.

We are put out with what we depend,
but must eat first before helping oxidise the earth.
Then wrap the others in a floatation cot.
Art is the limit of the empirical, a hashcake
is burning somewhere and a fistful of
weeping magic beans. So happy
that grown is combustible, the entelechy
made joules for the class is not,
so happily married. At the plummet
we have made our representations
besiege the represented and rep
resenters for honour
hey the task is serious: marathon irony
in which the man cradling his little son
is an instrument for a border

critique

This is a wonderful experiment,
by which you can carry fire in your hand,
or walk on fire, without being burned,
in Australia, reattaching yourself to native sump

by the action of no more than your mind.
With a little double
mallow, or white of egg,
spare yourself any damage
the *petit-pois* of a climate of general clinical
depression little peas line up in this positive
bent of your power, a sac, it's all in the mind
where decay is a recuperation the re-
verse likewise.

I am not enough and don't forget it
corrosive pop of the safety match my kin
will eat through the speaker's corner
of the face eventually: and the pure fire
is not within, but between, space lit
by the enmity and common fire of hope and envy
which one object kindles for the other:
the space can be pure so long as it remains empty
a carrier for the payload and the charity
acid that compresses the pupil
a hard knot of coal in the eye the small
nouns, the small resorts of the small poor, the little
hole in the eye, the little hole, the smallest corners
of man's triumph is a block of coal, a plug
eaten by the flammula vitae.

The body itself in repose
the magnesium to light a single photograph: raw
materials worth 25 francs if you can catch them.
We have no idea how to speak
clear truth, in thick of the doctrinal 600m danger-close
to take it in there and mass
fires on the little rabbity things, though fleet
of boot and sharp-jawed, they are susceptible to night

which they illuminate with the facts
embedded in their stinking fur so we can catch it
seeing outward with closed yes.

Light cast over our camp as if in day by reason
of the great mass of fire, and the brilliance of the light it shed,
the Four Moons of industry which delayed
the council for centuries to split
night with the criminals on the street we bought:
the celebrated luminous mists seen in 1783, 1831
and 1922, the limpid forever. Now
negation is so sweetly irresistible,
its price indexed to the high street and the aerial
though never knowingly undersold.
The Destruction of Language is proportionate,
and ratios of sleep and injury bound
between the newsbooks of anger and relief
to cause a minor ruckus on Today:
but never so tightly that the circulation stops.

Blooming and mating we turn on
step only once into view
with little yellow jewels burning on our eyebrows.
This is the reward, stepping out
into the innards whose inglorious
spit-roast makes the mute world present
outside a bereft and guilty place. In light of which
the infinite review burns out
wrapped in the whole,
design and act, shade and radiant
rides out the celestial outpouring
and seeks cover underground.

NOTE ON THE TEXT

Wildfire is a verse essay. It is trying to persuade us, to recognize that certain catastrophes and felicities are not inevitable. It concerns the history of incendiary devices, of the evolution of Greek fire from a divine secret which could sustain or destroy empires, into white phosphorus and napalm; the elliptical fires of the pre-Socratics, Aristotle's service to Alexander in the fashioning of pyrotechnics, the burning/blooming/mating bodies of G. H. Schubert and the self-feeding crowds of Elias Canetti; mechanisms to project fire, to make it burn on water and stick to wood and skin, to keep it off the walls of the besieged towns, and what those mechanisms (projection and defence) have done to geometry; the courts of fire, the legal chamber and the *hortus conclusus*, and the margins of ambiguity where it is lobbed with impunity; embedded nuggets and embedded reporters, the discovery of the chemical element, industrial tragedy, the resistance of the matchgirls at Bryant & May, the corruption of Quaker capitalists, washing powder and toothpaste. It is an etiology of metaphors, 'shake-n-bake' and whisky pete and phantom fury. It is also an argument about obscurity and illumination: WP does both, smokes the bright air and singes the night with trajectories. And so an interrogation of writing practices which fume as much as they enlighten.

The poem began as an attempt to bypass the vulnerability of writing to occasion. I'd got tired of susceptibility, ground in airy feeling. I wanted to write a forensic poem, one whose structure could accommodate an excess of social information. I was thinking about an aerial map, plotting contours in history and relaying the coordinates for a surgical strike. But I was tired of trying to position 'us' on the ground, like actors in real carnage, where being 'implicated' is also a way of sharing the spoils. I wanted not allegory but the recovery of material history, which tests the luxuries of myth and enjoys, but does not endorse, the luxuries of language.

The failure of my first effort to write such a poem, *Sweatbox*, showed me unable to cope with a rapidly unravelling history. That text attempted to plot the *Gilgamesh* epic, tablet by tablet, against the daily war (the second invasion of Iraq). Epic fragments were transported by Penguin Classics to a nook in London then back out to a pixellated field sewn with cluster bomblets and the shards of the Nemean lion. I busied myself at the British Museum, reading the blurbs, constellating fragments as a melancholic formal reminder of the fractures and losses in real-time reporting and in the dispersal of a living culture. But I couldn't keep up with the news, couldn't fit that fast degeneration to an epic impasto worth thousands of years. My appropriations showed through: the desire for wholeness implicit in the phrases airlifted from news bulletins; the desire for the right and the position to speak, for consensus and legitimacy of representation. The absence of those rights and places, the mourning echoes of the epic voice, turned the poem all tawdry ironic—better than a barbaric silence, but only just. Besides, everyone was doing *Gilgamesh* that year. I abandoned the project.

Although its aims are equally immodest, *Wildfire* was somehow more possible to stick to. Tracing the globalisation of a fire that feeds on life, it considers how ignition is missed, how many gallons of piss it takes to change a lightbulb, and how the fates of empires and individuals depend on accident. It follows as adventures in an ancient geography of perpetual fire become a world-defeating industry which drives all our consumption towards disaster. It examines the mutations of the body by exploitative labour, and the moral mutations which have become chronic to our engagement of the enemy. It also seeks to understand why the irenic languages of love, philosophy, and poetry are so indebted to fire; why we burn, melt, smoulder, are pierced by burning arrows from flaming eyes and in repose are lit by the light of nature.

The poem is throughout a commentary on itself, on culture as revolutionary praxis, on the transcendence still lurking in poetics which attribute to specific poems (or to themselves) the power to illuminate or obscure. But I hope that *Wildfire*'s position is not ironic. I don't want to fabricate a critique which spares me, in whose light I glow with ethical priority.

The integration of found texts is not meant to be seamless. I have used the open-ended single apostrophe to mark the beginning of quotations and not their end—the quoted text picks up what follows like a magnet. Tab spaces are another way of representing obliteration. These spaces suggest opportunities for pausing (if the poem is read silently or aloud), intervals in the argument or the history, and heuristic breaks which are not as absolute as stanza breaks but which do nonetheless shake off some of the logic of the preceding. These breaks may also be taken as space for critical thought.

What comes after can sometimes be an intruder.

The sources for the poem can be found on the Krupskaya website (www.krupskayabooks.com); a selected bibliography follows. I'm not trying to be pedantic. Inserting these texts into a poetic discourse can etherialize them, turn what were attempts at scientific, historical and philosophical precisions into mythopoeic spectacle. The bibliography should stabilize that tendency to sublimate. But more importantly, the poem stems from a desire to counter legal and extra-legal violence not with the naive pacifism that demands only (only?) a ban to the worst weapons or the end of all war—but with an understanding of our deep affections for fire, fires that consume, obliterate, stick and burn clear, that transform, catch, and outshine. Those fires bloom out of ancient history, dressed in the secrets of angels or the recipes of nature, illumine the mythic stumblings of chemistry and feed the engines of industrialization—where they were also resisted by workers united in their suffering. And all along, they crisp the civilized discourses into chiaroscuro delineations of right, wrong, inside, outside, privacy, publicity. If that is the case, we cannot wean ourselves from them by a simple willing towards peace, by reforming international instruments. A first step towards liberation from the brands and the boils of the most horrific dying is a recognition of the ancient complexity of the desire to burn.

What would make you throw yourself out?

SOURCES

ANCIENT and EARLY MODERN

Ancrene Wisse or the "Anchoresses' Guide" (Cambridge, Corpus Christi College, MS 402; c. 1225-1240).

Marcus Graecus, *Liber Ignium*, trans. J. R Partington in *A History of Greek Fire and Gunpowder* (Cambridge, 1960).

G. S. Kirk, J. E. Raven and M. Schofield, eds., *The Presocratic Philosophers*, 2nd ed. (Cambridge, 1983 [1957]).

Thomas May, trans., *Lucan's Pharsalia: or the Civill Warres of Rome, between Pompey the great, and Julius Caesar* (London, 1631).

Theophrastus, *De Igne*, ed. Victor Coutant (Assen, 1971).

Robert Boyle, *The Aerial Noctiluca: or Some New Phoenomena and a Process of a Factitious Self-Shining Substance* (London, 1680).

POETIC

Robert Browning, "An Epistle Containing the Strange Medical Experience of Karshish, the Arab Physician"

Ed Dorn, *Gunslinger*, Book III

John Keats, "Lamia"

Frank O'Hara, "Naphtha"

Charles Olson, "The Resistance" for Jean Riboud (1953), *Collected Prose*

Alfred Lord Tennyson, *In Memoriam*

Walt Whitman, "Song of the Redwood Tree"

MODERN

Jacob Abbott, "Military Pyrotechnics of Former Days: The story of Greek fire, the 'wonderful combustible'." *Harper's New Monthly Magazine* 39.229 (June 1869).

Georges Bataillle, Michel Leiris, Marcel Griaule, Carl Einstein and Robert Desnos, eds., 'Critical Dictionary', *Encyclopaedia Acephalica.*

Zayn Bilkadi, "The Oil Weapons: Ancient Oil Industries", *Aramco World* (Jan.-Feb. 1995): 22-7.

Elias Canetti, *Crowds and Power,* trans. Carol Stewart (London, 2000 [1962]).

Alfred Crosby, *Throwing Fire: Projectile Technology through History* (Cambridge, 2002).

John Emsley, *The Shocking History of Phosphorus, a Biography of the Devil's Element* (London, 2000).

R. J. Forbes, *Bitumen and Petroleum in Antiquity* (Leiden, 1964).

Robert Harris and Jeremy Paxman, *A Higher Form of Killing: The Secret Story of Chemical and Biological Warfare* (New York, 1982).

Sohail Hashmi and Steven Lee, eds., *Ethics and WMD* (Cambridge, 2004).

Alexander von Humboldt, 'Geognostic Phenomena', in *Cosmos: A Sketch of a Physical Description of the Universe,* vol. 1, trans. E. C. Otte (London, 1849).

Malvern Lumsden, *Incendiary Weapons* (Cambridge, MA, 1975).

Adrienne Mayor, *Greek Fire, Poison Arrows, and Scorpion Bomb: Biological and Chemical Warfare in the Ancient World* (New York, London and Woodstock, 2003).

Darrin Mortensen, 'Violence Subsides for Marines in Fallujah', *North County Times* (14 Sept. 2006).

David Park, *The Fire Within the Eye: A Historical Essay on the Nature and Meaning of Light* (Princeton, NJ, 1997).

James Riddick Partington, *A History of Greek Fire and Gunpowder* (Cambridge, 1960).

Thomas De Quincey, 'Suspiria de Profundis', in *Confessions of an English Opium-Eater and Other Writings*, ed. Grevel Lindop (Oxford, 1996).

Sigfrido Ranucci, dir., *Fallujah: The Hidden Massacre* [documentary] (RaiNews24, 8 Nov. 2005).

Paul Reynolds, 'White Phosphorous: Weapon on the Edge', *BBC News* (16 Nov. 2005).

Alex Roland, "Greek Fire", *MHQ: A Journal of Military History* 2 (Spring 1990): 16-19.

David Sansone, "Plutarch, Alexander, and the Discovery of Naphtha', *Greek, Roman and Byzantine Studies* 21 (1980): 63-74.

F. W. J. Schelling, *Ideas for a Philosophy of Nature,* trans. Errol E. Harris and Peter Heath (Cambridge, 1988).

Gotthilf Heinrich von Schubert, *Ansichten von der Nachtseite der Naturwissenschaft* [Views of the Nightside of Natural Science] (Dresden, 1808) and *Die Geschichte der Seele* [The History of the Soul] (Fifth ed, Stuttgart, J.C. Cotta, 1877), vol. 1.

W.H. Spears, Jr., *Greek Fire: The Fabulous Secret Weapon That Saved Europe* (1969).

John Maxson Stillman, *The Story of Alchemy and Early Chemistry* (New York, 1960).

Ashburton Thompson, *Free Phosphorous in Medicine* (1874).

Richard Threlfall, *The Story of 100 Years of Phosphorus Making, 1851-1951* (Oldbury, 1951).

Ernest Volkman, *Science Goes to War: The Search for the Ultimate Weapon, from Greek Fire to Star Wars* (New York, 2002).

ILLUSTRATIONS

The photograph on page 6 (burnt match, 'Pyrotechne') is by Mike Perkowitz.

The photographs on page 18 (WP falling on Fallujah, 'Chronic') are stills from *Fallujah: The Hidden Massacre*, a documentary by Sigfrido Ranucci (broadcast on RaiNews24, 8 November 2005).

The photograph on page 30 (the remains of Anna Martin following apparent spontaneous combustion, 'Meat') cannot be attributed; the engraving of a figure holding up his own skin is from Juan Valverde de Amusco's *Historia de la composicion del cuerpo humano* (Rome, 1560).

The picture on page 36 ('Alchemistry') is a detail from Joseph Wright of Derby, *The Alchemist in Search of the Philosophers Stone*.

The photograph on page 44 (oil fire, 'Crude') is by Jacques Descloitres, MODIS Rapid Response Team, NASA/GSFC.

The photograph on page 48 (M62 Tracer bullets, 'Thrown Fire') is from the website of River Valley Ordnance, Harvester, Missouri.

All other prohotographs are by the author.